Sacred Rose Blossom

Art and Poetry

Donna L Vincenti

Balboa Press books may be ordered through booksellers or by contacting:

Balboa Press
A Division of Hay House
1663 Liberty Drive
Bloomington, IN 47403
www.balboapress.com
844-682-1282

Because of the dynamic nature of the Internet, any web addresses or links contained in this book may have changed since publication and may no longer be valid. The views expressed in this work are solely those of the author and do not necessarily reflect the views of the publisher, and the publisher hereby disclaims any responsibility for them.

ISBN: 979-8-7652-3778-6 (sc)
ISBN: 979-8-7652-3779-3 (e)

Library of Congress Control Number: 2022923890

Print information available on the last page.

Balboa Press rev. date: 01/24/2023

Introduction

My awakening in 2012 led me to my healing journey.
In the 1980's my parents were diagnosed with a terminal illness
where I took care of them for eight years.

Through my awakening I started to look inward embracing it all
and healing. This led me to do energy healing work, write healing
poetry and paint.

This healing passage is dedicated to my parents, to you and to
finding the courage to love ourselves.

In God's grace and glory we find ourselves in his love, knowledge,
strength and wisdom.
The fortitude to make all things new.

I thank God, my angels and my family.

Donna L Vincenti

Contents

Embrace
your inner journey

Take a moment to meditate.

Let each one take you on a journey to embrace yourself and life's beauty.

Love, light and eternal blessings,

Donna L Vincenti

Inspiration

Infinite

Wishes

Spirit Guides

Spirit guides and leads

Works through us

A flute

A harp

A symphony

Melodies penetrating existence

Permeating dimensions and time

Embracing all that is

The fruit in all

Kissing life with your soul

Embrace

Hands

Color

God took my hands

His heart beats in it

To nurture and heal

To soothe and love

To share in all truth and glory

All that I am

His child

Hands

The tree wrapping its branches around me

Holding me

Cradling me

The life filling me from its root

Pulling the earth into and through

Grounding and Nurturing

Filling and Fueling

Soothing and Loving

Oh Tree of Mine

You are Divine

Embrace

Star

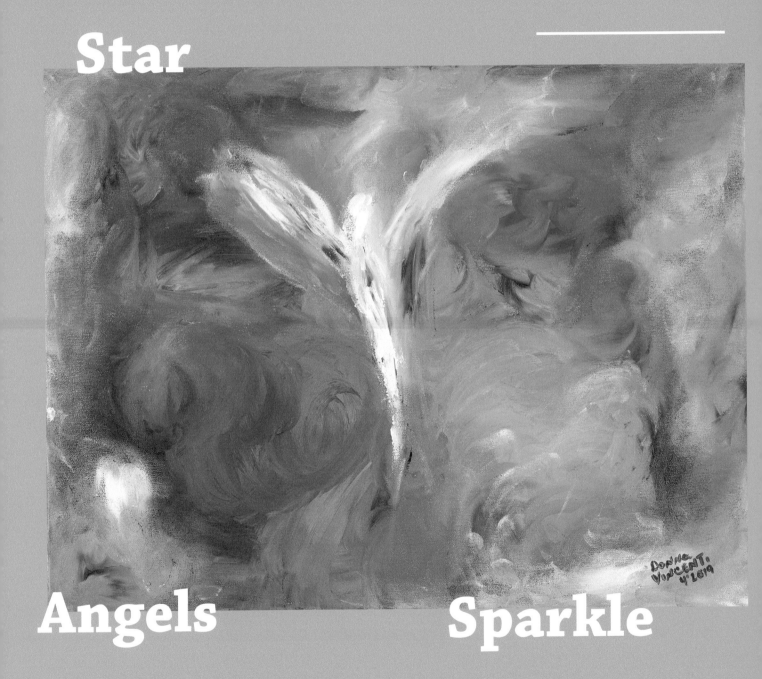

Angels

Sparkle

Infinity sparkles beyond

Help me to know my truth

Stand firm and rooted in all that I am

Filled with Love eternal

Light God is my source

He is me

Walking in Glory

All truth revealed

My angels dancing

Playfully guiding in passion and love

To surrender to all

The cosmic unfolding

The signs that fill my heart

A smile on my lips

The dance of life with every moment

Fruit Divine

Sparkles

Star travel

Stars travel in the night

Twinkling, Glimmering, Glittering

Shining in all glory

Shine your light with all your might

They sing Shine Shine Shine

In all your strength and glory

Be the shining star you are

God's grace and glory

You are made from and you are stardust

Shine your heavenly light

Sweet traveling star beings

Free to fly with all that you are

Glistening Golden Star

Illuminating my soul

Pouring light and truth into my heart

Penetrating all walls

Golden river flow

Inside me to shine in all magic

Majestically

God's being inside me piercing through all my cells

My being encapsulated

In the saviors love, guidance and protection

The Illuminated path

Unfolding before me

I walk in truth, comfort,

love, peace and joy

Golden star

Love

One

Sun

Dance with Me

Walk with Me

Sing with Me

Talk to Me

Listen to the Wind

The Song of birds

The Song of Soul

The divine love making of nature and life

Truly nourishing one another

Soul dancing in one euphoric orgasm inside

Of all Time and Space falls away

The only moment and truth is this

Orgasmic Love

Twins in the night

Flying by day

Flowers embrace us

Roots connected

Earth and Stars

We know who we are

The budding of all eternity

In this moment pure joy

Ecstasy, pulsating, penetrating

All time and space to all is now

The completeness wrapped in a moment of infinity

Twins in the night

Hearing, Listening to our souls

The cry and passion of the night

In God's love

Twin Love

Love Dive

Seductive Sea enveloping me

Wrapping lovingly

Wetness passion

Coolness penetrating

Soothing hugging

My soul my body infused with your strength

Fortitude deepening

Breathing deeply

Your soulful dance lingering on my lips

Traveling through me and in me

The river runs deep into ocean dives

Calm is the lake

Love is I

Trees embrace

One of truth

Lovers unite

In honest pure sacred journey

Karma all cleared

Paving new land

Clear slate

To grow to build

Paint, play, dance, love

My lover's arms

His smile shines

In my soul his heart I touch with my heart

Opening to the truth of our love on soul level

It cannot be denied nor run from

All truth penetrates form

The knowing powerful journey

of pure truth and real love

Coming home

Coming home

Heart caresses

One

To be one with all

Divine flows into me and through me

The trees the stars

The air the water

The earth

All inside pulsating in and through me

Holding, embracing and nurturing

Receiving and releasing

The smell of rain divine

The droplets so sweet and pure

From heaven

Touching the sacred earth

The droplets kissing the dirt

Grass reuniting in unity so blissful

Be in me as I am in you

We merge in unity

Always one

Oh Sun of Mine

You shine inside me

Filling me with your warmth and Love

You nurture my spirit, heart, mind, body and soul

Oh Sun of Mine

God

Heaven

Surrender

God Song

Sea drinking sky

Illuminating my soul

Sparkling

Twinkling

Space so divine

Birds singing

In glory

God's song

Love light peace in my heart

Father's Glory

God's Light

Rise from ashes

Pouring light in the holes of darkness

Light Pouring into each cell

As it dances in delight

God Speed

His work in the many

Truth

Purity

Kindness

Pouring out into the world

Let this be the way

God's Will

Every step God's will

Every word God's voice

Every thought is God

The angels hold us

Guide us

Carry us

Show us

All the rich abundance

Always is given to us

All is a gift

Every moment a gift

God supplies all needs

Shows us in the unfolding

Divine time

All that is

God's Love

How the sun feeds the earth and soul

Pouring into my body, heart, mind and soul

Drinking from thirsty well

How I drink and drink

The water from God's eternal well

Overflowing into me

Bearing fruit to share

To love, trust and honor myself

Is to Love, trust and honor my father

God almighty strength

Love, honor and glory is yours

I am yours

I am your child I am loved

Deeply and richly

How the birds sing and dance

Filling my soul with their magic, beauty, purity

All is God's Love

Open your heart and you will see

Heavenly Father

Glory shine in me

Your hand in mine

We walk sacred Road

Shining the love light and peace

Grace is my blessing

Your Strength is my virtue

Patience in all Seeds

Watered by You

Heaven is here

I heard him say

But only to look in your heart

Feel its beat, its rhythm pulsating

A waterfall cascading into the river of life inside

A river runs through us

Dear heavenly father

That we may be all you need

With hearts of gold, truth, purity,

wisdom, love and kindness

The courage to let our river run

Over and beyond

To swim in the ocean of your love

Heaven

Heavenly light

You fill my soul

The warmth on my skin

Drinking into my cells

Pouring into and feeding my soul

Pulsating through my blood

Flowing waters

Love and light

Dancing

Intertwined in each other's embrace

One with the Sun

Heavens Light

Surrender

Surrendering to God's will

Unfolding to divine source

All creation

Unfolding, Embracing, Releasing

Holding, Nurturing, Loving

Filled with God's strength and spirit

Listen to the call of my soul

Dance in the wind

Twirling with the trees

Singing with the birds

Filling up with life's divinity

The sun pouring life and light

The dancing moonbeams

The ocean washes over and through

Life's divine place

Sing and dance

Breathing in the heart body mind and soul

Eternal dance in God's delight

Garden

Rose

Earth

Tree Friends

Heavenly Tree

Rooted so Deep

You hold me in your Truth, Strength and Love

Thank you for Kissing my Spirit when we Hug

The Budding Tree

Birth and rebirth

The birds sing in joy

They dance and fly

In the beauty of heavenly sky

That embraces and holds us in its loving womb

Peace fills our souls in eternal now

The love of God

Filling within all divinity

We Reach high to sweet magical Stars

Touching as we become one

My branches your light beams

More than it seems

As we are cosmic streams

The bird's sweet song

Divine nectar in my soul

My ears like hearts

The rose drawing nectar from God's fruits

The bird's sweet song

Embraces the heart

Echoes inside

Traveling in all my cells

Bird Song

Gentle Breeze

Gentle loving breeze

How you love to tease

Fill me as you please

As we ride waves of ecstasy

You sooth my skin ever so soft

Caress my body, heart and soul

Ease my mind to a Summer's Day

Wrapped in my Lover's arms

Gentle breeze

Stay with me

As you please

Linger in the Sun

Filling me with Strength

The sun's warmth and glory

Shining inside and through me

Dripping honey from my lips

Sun soaked in its love

Illuminating the pure ecstasy inside me

Filling me with truth, wisdom, love and fortitude

Brightening my soul to share and expand

Guiding my path

Lighting the way step by step

Filled with God's Light, Love, Peace and Glory

In the Garden I walk

The Garden

Earth Quench

Rose covered Earth

Love pouring through

Quenching your thirsty soul

Drink and know you are loved

Sun Drenched Love

Pouring inside me

Rainbow drops fill me

Moon Rays flow in me

Paradise is inside

New Earth emerging

New Earth

The Rose

The Rose filled with all God's love and glory

Petals soft like dew

A river of pulsating love flowing through

Fragrance to fill the soul

Velvety rich succulent aroma filling all of me

The stem rooted into the earth

Flowing up into me

Petals opening, blooming, blossoming inside me

Filling me at the very core

Opening into every crevice and cell

Filling me with rivers of love to share

Printed in the United States
by Baker & Taylor Publisher Services